WHERE in the WiLD?

Camouflaged Creatures Concealed...and Revealed

Ear-Tickling Poems by David M. Schwartz and Yael Schy | Eye-Tricking Photos by Dwight Kuhn

TRICYCLE PRESS

BERKELEY

CAN YOU FiND ME?

TURN TO THE LAST PAGE IF YOU'RE STUMPED.

Imagine that you are an animal in the wild trying to avoid a prowling predator. If it can't find you, it can't eat you.

Now imagine that you are the predator, silently hunting for prey. If your prey does not see you, you can catch it and eat it.

Whether an animal is looking for something to eat or trying to avoid being eaten—or both—it will probably survive longer if it blends into its environment. That's why some creatures hide with their colors. It's called "camouflage." An animal can be so well camouflaged that it practically vanishes in plain sight. To stay camouflaged, some creatures change their appearance from one minute to another or from one season to the next.

See if you can find the camouflaged animals photographed in their natural habitats. The poems will give you hints. When you think you have found a hidden animal—or if you give up!—open the flap to see "where in the wild" it really is. Then read on to find out more about these amazing animals and their vanishing acts.

Wary Eyes

Wary eyes . . .

Ears are keen . . .

Sniff the air . . .

Seldom seen . . .

Crouching low . . .

In the brush . . .

Standing still . . .

Watching, hush . . .

Darkness falls . . .

On the prowl . . .

Rising moon . . .

Yip and HOOOWWWWWWLLLLL

LIFT TO
FIND ME!

Coyote

The howl of the coyote is a well-known song of the West, but coyotes are more often heard than seen. These intelligent, bushy-tailed cousins of domestic dogs are most active at night when they yip and howl. The scientific name of the coyote, *Canis latrans*, means "barking dog."

A coyote's excellent senses of smell, vision, and hearing help it find prey and avoid danger. With a drab reddish-gray coat and the instinct to stand still when frightened, coyotes are easily overlooked. Once the threat has passed, they may silently dash away, running up to forty miles per hour.

Coyotes once lived only on the western prairies of the United States. Some Native Americans call them "little wolf." Now they thrive all over North America, including areas where millions of people live. As suburbs and cities take over fields and forests, more and more coyotes encounter humans. But most people never know it.

Grayish, Greenish

Grayish, greenish, blackish tree
The colors you see are the colors of me.

Grayish, greenish, blackish bark
I'm bumpy and blotchy, part light and part dark.

Grayish, greenish — what do I hear?
A sound in the branches that's coming too near!

Grayish, greenish, blackish — YIKES!
What if he saw me — what if he strikes?

Grayish, greenish — what do I feel?
OH NO! HE HAS FOUND ME, I'LL SOON BE HIS . . .

LIFT TO
FIND ME!

Gray Tree Frog

If you hear a high trill in the trees, it might be a bird or an insect. Or it might be a tree frog.

Most frogs live in water, but some species live in trees, leaping from branch to branch, gripping the wood with the sticky suction pads at the ends of their toes. A tree frog's long tongue is also sticky. Zzzaaap. Bye-bye, fly!

Brightly colored tree frogs have poisonous skin that no predator wants to eat. Their colors advertise their poisons. "Watch out!" they seem to be saying. "You don't want to eat me!" But many kinds of tree frogs are not toxic, and they would make a fine meal for a snake or an owl. For these frogs, their defense is in their camouflage.

Gray tree frogs have rough, bumpy gray-green skin with dark patches. Against trees blotched with moss and lichens, they practically disappear. When a gray tree frog moves from a dark trunk to lighter-colored leaves, its skin turns light green. Most of the time, the gray tree frog's camouflage works. But once in a while, the predator's eyes are better than the tree frog's disguise!

Spots

Spots, spots,
we've got lots—
not checks or stripes
or polka dots.

Not pointy stars
or red race cars.
Not rainbow arcs
or great white sharks!

In this field of white clover
we're covered all over
with spotty white patches
so no one can catch us!

On weak, wobbly legs
we can't run away,
so we'll hide with our spots
till we're bigger some day!

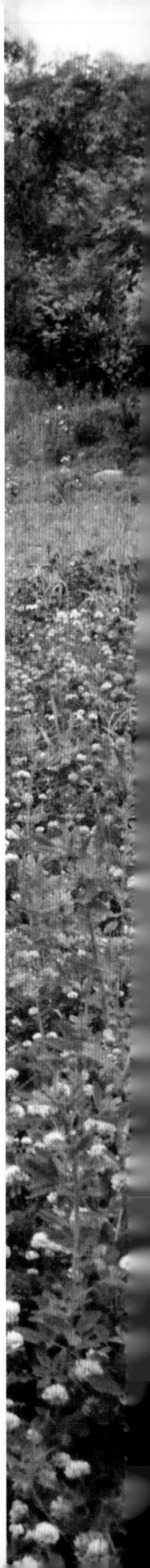

LIFT TO
FIND ME!

Fawns

Within a few hours of its birth, a baby deer can stand up and graze in the meadow. But with its weak and spindly legs, it may not be able to outrun predators. The fawn is safer if it can hide from danger instead.

The spots on these fawns' coats make them hard to find. Imagine what this field looks like to a predator. Coyotes, bobcats, and other members of the dog and cat families only see in black-and-white. They may not notice the brown, spotted fur of a small fawn against a field of green grass, especially when the field is dotted with wildflowers.

By the end of their first year, these two young deer will be swift runners. They will no longer need to hide, so the spots on their coats will fade away.

Silent and Still

I'm silent and still, till I leap out and pounce.

Even prey twice my size I can easily trounce.

To feast on a rabbit, a rat, or a mole,

I stalk it, then capture it deep in its hole.

In the warm summer months, my coat is dark brown.

Then as winter arrives, I don a white gown.

I can hide in full view, without caution or fear.

In this snow-covered field, I just disappear.

LIFT TO
FIND ME!

Weasel

Alert and watchful, a snow-white weasel perches on a dry stalk, waiting to pounce on unsuspecting prey. Weasels are small, speedy, and strong. They are fearless hunters who can take on animals much larger than themselves. Pound for pound, they are among the most ferocious of predators.

Some weasels have different wardrobes for summer and winter. As days grow short and brisk in northern areas, the short-tailed weasel, or ermine, trades its chocolate brown coat for a white one. Only its black-tipped tail stays dark. Now the small predator can lie in wait or prowl silently in the snow, unnoticed by the rodent who might become its next meal. A weasel eats almost half its weight in food each day. (This is like a 100-pound person eating fifty pounds of hamburger every day—that's 200 quarter-pound burgers!) Imagine how many more mice and rats would be running around if it weren't for weasels!

Because of their cunning and disguise, weasels are rarely seen by humans. Yet, every day of the year they are out in the grasslands, woods, marshes, and fields doing the important work of predators.

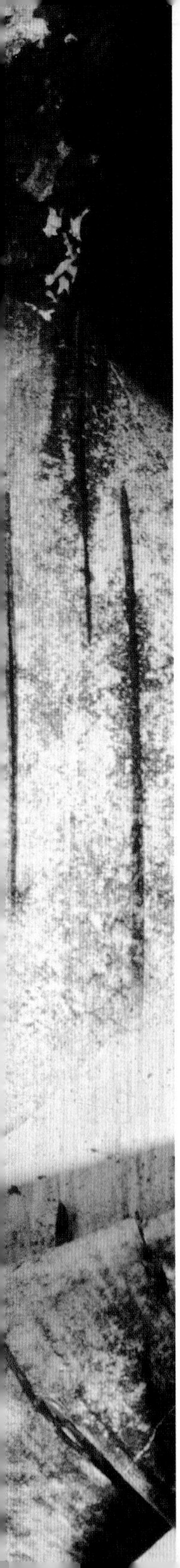

Wings Outspread

flitting

darting

zigzag flight

blurry wing beats

in the night

resting

outspread

wings of white

blend with birch bark

by day's light

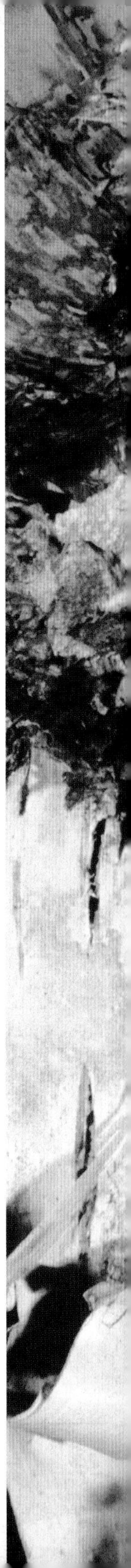

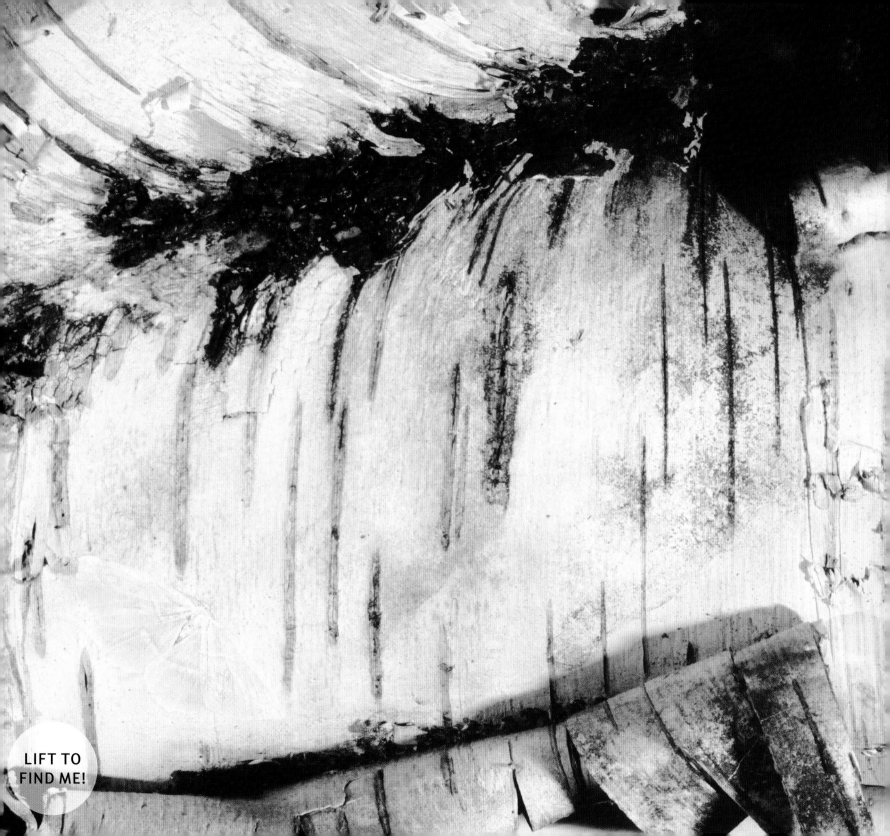

LIFT TO
FIND ME!

Moth

In England more than a century ago, a kind of geometer called the pepper moth had light–colored wings that were "peppered" with dark specks. Pepper moths hid well on light-barked trees blotched with grayish lichens. After factories began to pollute the air in industrial cities, soot from the smokestacks darkened the tree bark. In some areas, the moth populations evolved to be darker, matching the trees on which they rested. By doing this, they continued to evade birds looking for a mothy meal.

Moths are nocturnal—they fly and feed at night. Some are expert fliers who can evade even the fastest bats. But during the day, a resting moth is easy prey for hungry birds. By blending into its surroundings, a moth that is well-camouflaged can sleep undisturbed.

The larvae of certain moths are called inchworms. These moths are known as "geometers," meaning "earth measurers." As a larva inches its way along a twig, it seems to be measuring it.

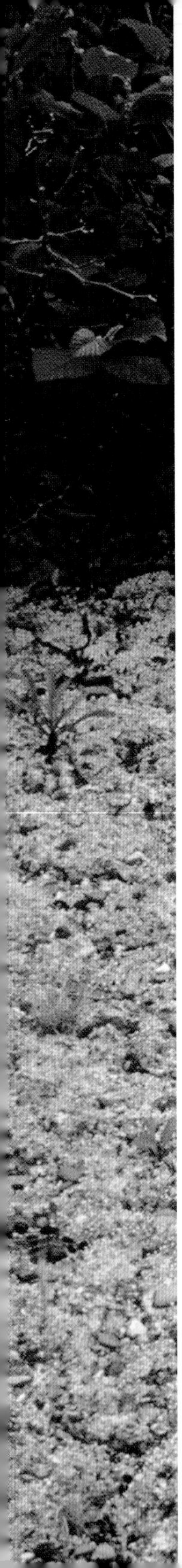

Speckled Treasures

speckled treasures lie
    bare upon the pebbled bank
        fragile life within

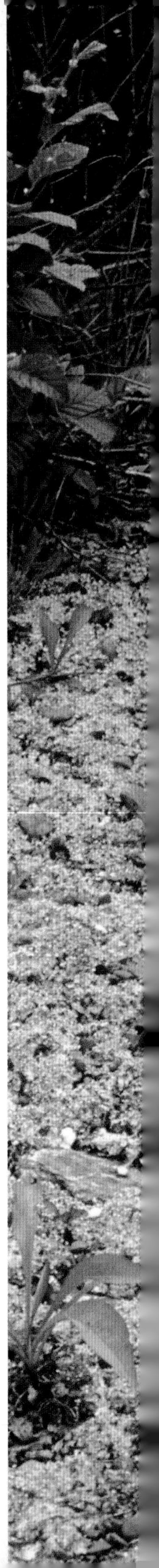

LIFT TO
FIND ME!

Killdeer Eggs

Where does a mother bird lay her eggs? In a nest of twigs, perhaps, or in the protective hole of a tree or cliff. But there are also birds who lay their eggs in open places. A nest would catch the eye of a predator, leading it to the precious eggs. Shorebirds lay their speckled eggs directly on a stony beach or riverbank. The colors and pattern of the eggs match the pebbly ground. A raccoon walking on the beach or a gull flying overhead would probably pass right by. No eggs for breakfast today!

The killdeer is a shorebird but it often lives inland, far from shore. Like other shorebirds, killdeer mothers nest in stony places where their dappled eggs are hard to see. But the killdeer has another trick as well. If a predator comes too close to a killdeer sitting on her eggs, the mother flies off. "Kill-DEER! Kill-DEER!" she shrieks, distracting the hungry hunter. Then the mother drops to the ground, holding one wing at an awkward angle. Fooled into thinking that the bird's wing is broken, the predator chases her. But as it nears she takes off, again screaming, "Kill-DEER! Kill-DEER! Kill-DEER!" By now, the confused predator is far from the eggs, which continue to lie safely in plain sight.

Motionless

Motionless on yellow blooms I hide, blending in so well I can't be spied.

Poised to strike, for days or weeks I lie, till a careless fly alights nearby.

Lashing out, I quickly snatch the fly, pierce its back, and swiftly suck it dry.

Once again, I lie in wait for prey. Camouflage and patience are my way.

LIFT TO
FIND ME!

Crab Spider

Crab spiders, so named because they move sideways like a crab, are masters of ambush because they are masters of camouflage. On yellow petals, a yellow crab spider is nearly invisible. As spring turns to summer and summer to fall, the crab spider scuttles to new hunting grounds, often changing colors to match the flowers of a new season.

Some spiders spin webs to trap their prey. Others take mighty leaps and pounce upon their prey. Crab spiders sit on leaves or flowers and wait . . . and wait . . . and wait. With its powerful forelegs, a crab spider can grab any insect unlucky enough to land within striking distance. Nectar-feeding bees are its frequent victims. The spider's quick, venomous bite kills the bee before it can defend itself. Soon the predator will suck out the bee's insides, leaving nothing but an empty exoskeleton.

Eyes on One Side

I taste so delicious, the fisherman wishes
to catch me and make me his meal.
So upward I look, in fear of a hook
attached to a rod and a reel.

I can turn tan or brown, as I lie belly down
on the sea floor, through low and high tide.
Even stranger than that, I am totally flat,
with both of my eyes on one side!

I once swam about, like a bass or a trout,
till I made my home here on the bottom.
When a small fry swims by, I am fast on the fly,
and with one sudden move . . . I GOT 'IM!

LIFT TO
FIND ME!

Flounder

A flounder has covered itself with sand. It lies flat on the ocean floor, with only its bulging eyes sticking out. Spotting a small fish, the flounder darts out to catch it.

This fish's sharp vision notices the color of the seabed, and changes its skin color to match. In a matter of minutes, it can go from tan to gray or brown to black, while its belly stays white.

Flounders are not born flat. As larvae, they have an eye on each side of the head and swim about just like other fish. But through metamorphosis, the larva's body flattens. As it grows into an adult, one eye migrates to the other side of its head and the fish moves to the ocean bottom. The flounder shown here is called a winter flounder or lemon sole. It has both eyes on the right side of its body.

A larger flatfish, the summer flounder, has its eyes on the left side.

A flounder's unusual body shape and its ability to change color keep it well hidden, both from predators and from unsuspecting prey. But camouflage will not prevent it from being fooled by a worm dangling on the end of a hook!

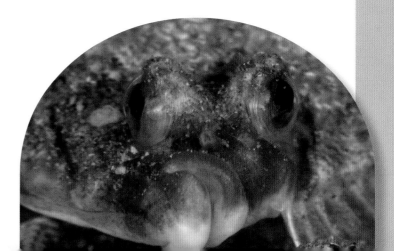

Serpentine

Silently gliding, slithering, sliding, in the grass hiding,

coiled and cunning, swift and stunning, on a rock sunning,

long and lean, smooth and green, serpentine.

LIFT TO
FIND ME!

Green Snake

With its smooth green scales, this snake easily blends in with grass and other plants of the meadow, forest, or garden. Camouflage helps it avoid becoming lunch for a coyote or a badger—and camouflage also helps the snake find its own lunch. Spiders, grasshoppers, worms, and caterpillars may not see it coming.

The nonpoisonous green snake is not as secretive as many other snakes, but when you approach one, it will likely slip away for a short distance, then stop and sway gently, like grass blowing in the breeze.

In the winter, green snakes hibernate in burrows and rock crevices. With warmer spring temperatures, they come out of hiding to mate. The females lay soft, leathery eggs in protected places, such as hollow logs. Parents do not guard their eggs or look after their young. When a baby snake is ready to hatch, it cuts through the shell with a sharp egg tooth on the front of its head. Then it wriggles out and slithers off into the world.

Vagabond

I'm now a forest vagabond,
but I was born within a pond.
I hatched from one of many eggs.
I swam around—I had no legs.

I grew and changed to look like this—
they call that metamorphosis.
With lungs to breathe and legs to stand,
I walk about upon dry land.

If you should see me on a hike,
you may think I'm lizard-like.
But I'm no reptile, think again—
I'm really an amphibian!

LIFT TO
FIND ME!

Red-spotted Newt

Newts, like all salamanders, are amphibians, which in Greek means "double life." They begin life in the water, and then change into a new form to live on land. This process is called "metamorphosis."

Red-spotted newts hatch from eggs laid in the ponds and streams of eastern North America. The larvae look like chubby greenish-brown fish with long tails, no legs, and bright red spots. They breathe through gills. After a few weeks, the larvae begin to grow legs and lungs. Their smooth, velvety skin turns orange or reddish brown, and they crawl out of the water to live in the forest. During this phase, they are called "red efts." Because efts and adult newts look so different, for many years scientists did not realize they were the same species!

The eft's skin contains toxic chemicals, and its bright color warns many predators away. Others, including raccoons, don't seem to mind the toxins. But on a forest floor littered with bright red leaves, a predator would have a hard time spotting a bright red eft.

After several years, the forest-dwelling eft goes through another metamorphosis. It sheds its skin and turns olive green. Its legs shrink and its tail thickens. Now it is an adult newt, and it returns to the water, possibly the very same pond where it hatched years ago. There it breeds and lays eggs, and the life cycle of the newt begins anew.

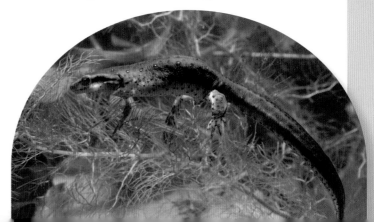

HERE
I AM!

To Leo, my friend and fellow explorer of places where wild things hide.—D.M.S.

To my nieces and nephews, Ilana, Oren, Marin, and Trevor, who love the wild outdoors.—Y.S.

To my granddaughter, Emma.—D.K.

Tricycle Press and the Tricycle Press colophon are registered trademarks
of Random House, Inc.

Schwartz, David M.
Where in the wild? : camouflaged animals concealed and revealed :
ear-tickling poems / by David M. Schwartz and Yael Schy ; eye-tricking photos by Dwight Kuhn.
p. cm.
1. Animals--Juvenile literature. 2. Camouflage (Biology)--Juvenile
literature. I. Schy, Yael. II. Title.
QL49.S2753 2007
590--dc22
2006101406

ISBN 978-1-58246-207-3

Printed in China

Design by Melissa Brown
Typeset in Grilled Cheese and Lisboa

13 12 11 10 9 8 7 6 5 4

First Edition